RICE DISHES

Colophon

© 2003 Rebo International b.v., Lisse, The Netherlands

www.rebo-publishers.com – info@rebo-publishers.com

Original recipes and photographs: © Ceres Verlag, Rudolf-August Oetker KG, Bielefeld, Germany

Design and layout: Minkowsky Graphics, Enkhuizen, The Netherlands

Cover design: Minkowsky Graphics, Enkhuizen, The Netherlands

Translation and typesetting: American Pie, London, UK and Sunnyvale, California, USA

Proofreading: Jarmila Pešková Škraňáková, Joshua H. Joseph

ISBN 90 366 1624 7

RICE DISHES

rice recipes from around the world for

creative cooking

REBO
PUBLISHERS

Foreword

Rice is probably the most important ingredient of the daily meal throughout the world. In China, it is eaten three times a day. Italy has its risotto rice, while India and Pakistan have basmati rice. Rice is very nutritious and much lighter than, say, pasta. Moreover, rice is very tasty and unbelievably versatile.

We have selected the most delicious rice recipes for this book. Some examples are *Wedding Rice* and *Norwegian Red Snapper Fillet with Wild Rice Cakes*. Paella is also included and you have the option of 4 different rice dishes to eat with it. Bon appetit!

Abbreviations

Contents

All measurements conform to American and European measurement system. For easier cooking, the American cup measurement is used throughout the book.

tbsp = tablespoon

tsp= teaspoon

oz = ounce

lb = pound

°F = degrees Fahrenheit

°C = degrees Celsius

g = gram

kg = kilogram

Method

Wash the chicken under running water. Clean the inside of the chicken and place it, with the heart and neck, into a deep pot of salted boiling water. As broth returns to boil, skim the surface.

Wash and chop the vegetables, and add them to the soup. Peel the onion and add it to the pot.

Cover and simmer the chicken in the broth for about 90 minutes. Strain the soup and add salt to taste.

Remove the meat from the bones, discard the skin, and cut the meat into small pieces.

Add the asparagus pieces, rice, and chicken pieces to the broth. Reheat, skimming the surface with absorbent paper towel to remove excess fat. Sprinkle with minced parsley before serving.

Ingredients

1 boiling fowl (around 2½ lb/1.2kg)

6 cups boiling salted water

1 bunch soup vegetables
(carrot, turnip, rutabaga)

salt

1 medium onion

2 cups cooked asparagus

½ cup cooked long-grain rice

2 tbsp minced parsley

Chicken Soup with Rice

Method

Peel and chop the onions and sauté them in butter until translucent. Add the rice, mix well, and continue cooking for 5 minutes, stirring. Add the vegetable broth, bring to a boil, and cook for 20 minutes. Season with salt, pepper, and grated nutmeg.

Clean and dice the carrots. Add them to soup and cook for 5 minutes.

Squeeze the juice of two of the lemons and add to the soup. Mix the crème fraîche into the liquid and bring to a boil.

Rinse the untreated lemon in hot water and cut into small slices. Pour the soup into 4 bowls and garnish with the lemon slices.

Rice and Carrot Soup with Lemon

Ingredients

1 small onion	½ tsp white pepper
2 tbsp butter	½ tsp grated nutmeg
⅓ cup long-grain rice	3 carrots
4 cups vegetable broth	3 lemons, 1 untreated
1 tsp salt	3 tbsp crème fraîche

Method

Heat the oil in a big pot. Peel and chop the onions and sauté them in the oil.

Wash the leek under cold running water and drain well. Cut the leek into slices and add these

to the onions, sautéing them together for 5 minutes.

Rinse the rice in cold running water, drain well, then add to the vegetables. Add the vegetable

broth, then the bayleaf and rosemary. Season well with salt, pepper, and grated nutmeg. Reduce

the heat and simmer the soup on low heat for 20-25 minutes.

Mix the milk and flour, add to the soup, and cook for 5 minutes.

Mix the egg yolk with yogurt. Remove the soup from the burner and thicken it with the yogurt mix.

Season the rice soup once again. Before serving, mix in the rinsed and finely chopped mint.

Rice Soup with Mint

Ingredients

2 tbsp olive oil

1 onion

1 leek

⅔ cup rice

2 cups vegetable broth

1 bayleaf

1 sprig rosemary

⅔ cup milk

1 tbsp all-purpose flour

2-3 egg yolks

⅔ cup yogurt

1 bunch fresh mint

freshly ground pepper

grated nutmeg

salt

soups with rice

Method

Peel and mince the onion and sauté in hot oil. Sprinkle with the flour and curry powder, simmer for 2-3 minutes, then add the meat broth.

Wash the rice, add to the broth, and cook for around 20 minutes, or until the rice is soft. Flavor with the sherry.

Beat an egg yolk with sour cream and thicken the soup with it. Remove from the pan, and serve immediately.

Ingredients

1 small onion

2-3 tbsp oil

2 tbsp all-purpose flour

1 tsp curry powder

4 cups meat broth

3 tbsp short-grain Italian rice

2-3 tbsp sherry

1 egg yolk

3-4 tbsp sour cream

Indian Rice Soup

Method

Add the rice to the boiling water, cook according to the package instructions, and strain in a colander.

Wash the peas and cook for about 10 minutes in ½ cup salted boiling water. Discard any wilted leaves from the Chinese cabbage and cut the cabbage in half. Cut out the core and wash the cabbage. Shred and strain the cabbage well.

Mix the ingredients for the salad and arrange on small plates. Skin the chicken, cut into strips, and arrange on top of the salad.

To make the salad dressing: vigorously beat the vinegar, mustard, sugar, salt, and pepper. Add the oil, drop by drop, and continue beating until the mixture is thick and creamy.

Add the lemon juice, stir, and pour over the salad. Let the flavors mingle for 30 minutes before serving.

Summertime Rice Salad

Ingredients

1 cup long-grain rice

4 cups boiling salted water

1½ cups shelled peas (around

1lb 9oz/675g in the shell)

1 Chinese (Napa) cabbage (around 8oz/450g)

1¾ cups cooked chicken

For the salad dressing

3 tbsp white wine vinegar

3 tsp hot mustard

½ tsp sugar; salt

freshly ground pepper

6 tbsp lemon juice

6 tbsp oil

Method

Place the rice in boiling salted water and cook for around 20 minutes. Drain the water and let the rice cool.

Combine the mayonnaise, crème fraîche, curry powder, lemon juice, sugar, ginger, and cayenne pepper.

Peel the apple and cut into pieces. Cut the pineapple into small pieces. Add the rice to the curry sauce. Cover the pot and simmer until the sauce is absorbed.

Add the shrimp. Toast the pumpkin seeds in a dry skillet and sprinkle them over the salad.

Ingredients

⅔ cup long-grain rice

2 cups salted water

2 tbsp mayonnaise

2 tbsp crème fraîche

1-2 tbsp curry powder

2 tbsp lemon juice

½ tsp sugar

¼ tsp grated ginger root

pinch cayenne pepper

1 large apple

3 slices fresh pineapple

⅔ cup bay shrimp

3 tbsp pumpkin seeds (pepitas)

Rice Salad with Shrimp

Method

Bring a pot of salted water to boil and cook the rice for around 40 minutes. Strain the rice and allow to cool.

Soak the raisins in water. Peel the apples, cut them in half, remove the cores, and dice them. Also dice the pineapple slices. Drain the raisins.

Add the apple and pineapple cubes as well as the raisins and slivered almonds to the rice.

To make the dressing: mix the heavy cream with the rest of the ingredients.

Mix the dressing with the salad ingredients and let the flavors mingle. Season again with salt and pepper before serving.

Ingredients

For the rice

2 cups water

⅔ cup brown or white rice

3 tbsp raisins

1 medium tart apple

2 slices fresh pineapple

3 tbsp slivered, blanched almonds

salt

For the dressing

1¾ cups sour cream

2 tbsp mango chutney

1 tbsp curry powder

2 slices candied ginger

1 lemon, juice squeezed

freshly ground pepper

Rice Salad with Pineapple

Method

Bring a pot of salted water to boil, add the rice, and stir well. Return to boil and cook at a rolling boil for around 30 minutes. Strain the rice, rinse it in cold water, and let it drain well.

Clean and slice the green onions. Rinse and drain well. Separate the lettuce leaves and cut them into strips. Wash the lettuce and drain or dry in a lettuce spinner. Slice the whitefish and ham into strips.

Mix the eggs, ketchup, and ginger sauce add this mixture with the green onion to the rice. Season with salt and pepper.

Reheat the mixture in a saucepan and let thicken. Add the whitefish and lettuce strips and decorate with the ham strips.

Ingredients

2 cups salted water

1 cup whole-grain rice

2 green onions (scallions)

1 head lettuce

4oz/115g smoked whitefish

4oz/115g country ham

4 eggs

1 tbsp tomato ketchup

1 tsp ginger juice

freshly ground pepper

salt

Whole-grain Rice with Ham and Whitefish

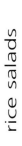

Method

Soak the mushrooms in warm water for 20 minutes. Cook the rice in boiling water for around 20 minutes. Stew the peas in lightly salted boiling water for around 3 minutes; strain, and keep warm.

Beat the eggs lightly with a little salt. Heat 1 tablespoon of oil in a wok, add the eggs, and stir until the eggs set. Keep the eggs warm.

Rinse the pork fillet in running water. Pat dry and cut into cubes. Cut the ham into strips. Strain the soaked mushrooms and cut into small pieces. Heat 2 tablespoons of oil in the wok and stir-fry the mushrooms. Add the pork and cook for around 5 minutes.

Add the ham and let it cook, stirring constantly, for around 2 minutes. Add the shrimp and cook for around 1 minute. Season with ketchup, remove from the wok, and keep warm.

Peel and chop an onion. Heat the wok and sauté the chopped onion until it is translucent. Add the strained rice, peas, scrambled eggs, meat, mushrooms, ham, and shrimp.

Mix everything together and add salt and pepper to taste.

Ingredients

1 tbsp dry Chinese mushrooms (wood ears)

1 cup rice

⅔ cup frozen peas

2 cups salted water

2 eggs

salt

7 tbsp oil

4oz/115g lean pork fillet

4oz/115g cooked ham

⅔ cup bay shrimp

1 tbsp tomato ketchup

1 onion

freshly ground pepper

Five Color Rice

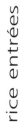

rice entrées

Method

Boil the rice for the rice cookies in salted water for 35-40 minutes. Strain and cool. Clean the leek thoroughly and cut into thin slices.

Melt 2 tablespoons of the butter and fry the leek. Remove the leek and let it cool.

Mix the rice, leek, and egg, then season with salt and pepper. Melt the rest of the butter and use a tablespoon to transfer small portions of the rice to a skillet. Press the rice portions flat, brown them on both sides for 2 minutes, and keep them warm.

Rinse the fish fillet in cold running water, pat dry, and sprinkle with lemon juice. Season with salt and pepper, pressing the pepper into the fish.

Melt the butter, fry each side for around 8 minutes, and keep warm.

For the sauce: peel and finely cut the shallots. Melt half the butter and sauté the shallot until it is glazed. Beat in the flour then moisten with the wine.

Bring the sauce to a rolling boil. Add the rest of the butter, the mustard, and cream, and let the sauce simmer for around 3 minutes. Season with salt and pepper.

Arrange the fillets together with the wild rice cookies and sauce on a plate.

Ingredients

For the wild rice cookies

6 tbsp wild rice

4 cups salted water

½ leek

3 tbsp butter

1 egg

salt

freshly ground pepper

For the fish

4 red snapper fillets (around 7oz/200g)

1 lemon, juice squeezed

4 tbsp butter

Red Snapper Fillet with Wild Rice Cookies

For the champagne-mustard sauce

2 shallots

2oz/50g butter

1 tbsp all-purpose flour

1 cup dry white wine

2 tbsp champagne mustard

1 cup heavy cream

Serving suggestion

Radicchio salad or leeks.

rice entrées

Method

Put the crawfish in boiling water, peel the onion and slice it in half, then add half to the crawfish. Wash the parsley and leek, cut the leek into pieces and add these together with the parsley and bayleaf to the crawfish. Cook for a few minutes, remove the crawfish, and let cool.

Shell the crawfish, reserving the shells. Grind the shells in a mortar, return them to the cooking liquid and simmer over low heat for around 15 minutes.

Heat 3 tablespoons of butter with the oil, mince the reserved onion half, add to the skillet, and sauté until brown. Rinse and drain the rice.

Strain the crawfish cooking liquid and add it to the skillet. Add the rice as soon as it is boiling. Season with pepper, salt, and the peeled and crushed garlic clove. Simmer for around 20 minutes. Mix the rest of the butter into the rice. Arrange the cooked crawfish on top and garnish with basil.

Crawfish Risotto

Ingredients	
1lb/450g crawfish	1 bayleaf
3 cups water	⅔ cup butter
1 small onion	2 tbsp olive oil
1 bunch parsley	1¾ cups round-grain (arborio) rice
1 leek	1 clove garlic
	fresh basil

Method

Peel and mince the onions. Heat the oil and fry the minced onions in a saucepan. Scald the tomatoes in boiling water (don't let them cook), and rinse them in cold water. Skin, discard the core, and cut them into quarters. Deseed, dice and add the flesh to the onions.

Wash the rice, add to the mixture, and sauté, stirring until the rice is glazed. Add half the broth and half the tomato juice, season with salt, pepper, and oregano. Bring to a boil and then simmer gently. When the liquid has evaporated, add the rest of the tomato juice and the broth, one tablespoon at a time.

Cook on low heat for around 25 minutes until the risotto has a creamy consistency.

Stir the cheese into the rice and reheat. Season with salt and pepper to taste.

Ingredients

2 onions	1 cup vegetable broth
5 tbsp oil	oregano leaves
3 tomatoes	3 tbsp grated yellow cheese
1 cup round-grain rice	freshly ground pepper
2 cups tomato juice	salt

Risotto Pomodori

Tip

Serve Risotto Pomodori with stir-fried meat

or fish goujons or

with a mixed salad for a vegetarian meal.

Method

Wash and strain the beansprouts and bamboo shoots. Wash the leeks and slice them into rings.

Heat the sesame oil in a wok. Fry the leek rings, beansprouts, and bamboo shoots. Add the rice and shrimp and sauté (the rice may change color). Season with salt, pepper, katjap, and sambal.

Rinse pat dry, and cut the chives into small rings. Beat the eggs with the chives, pour over the rice and let it curd vigorously.

Added ingredient:

Krupuk (Indonesian fish or seafood chips)

If unavailable, add Chinese shrimp crackers. The katjap can be replaced by a mixture of soy sauce and Thai or Vietnamese fish sauce.

Indonesian Fried Rice

Ingredients

1¾ cups beansprouts	salt
1½ cups fresh or canned bamboo sprouts	freshly ground pepper
1 small leek	katjap (Indonesian soy sauce)
4 tbsp sesame oil	sambal oelek (Indonesian hot spice)
1¾ cups long-grain rice, cooked	1 bunch chives
1 cup bay shrimp	4 eggs

rice entrées

Method

Defrost the shrimp according to the package directions. Rinse the tomatoes under cold running water, pat dry, halve, and cut off the stems. Cut the yellow bell pepper in half; remove the stems, seeds, and ribs. Rinse the pepper, cut it into large pieces and scald in salted boiling water for 3-4 minutes. Drain in a colander and peel off the skin.

Peel 4 garlic cloves and cut them in half. Rub the mushrooms with kitchen paper to clean them and thread all the ingredients on metal or wooden skewers.

Peel 2 garlic cloves and press them through a garlic press. Melt the butter and add the pressed garlic, lemon juice, salt, and sugar. Baste the kabobs with this mixture. Broil the kabobs on a broiler pan lined with aluminum foil or grill them on a barbecue, allowing at least 2 minutes on each side. **Serve** with boiled rice.

Shrimp Kabobs

Ingredients

For the kabobs	For the garlic butter
12 frozen bay shrimps	2 cloves garlic
(headless, with shells)	2 tbsp butter
4 salad tomatoes	1 tbsp lemon juice
1 yellow bell pepper	salt; sugar
salted water	**Tip**
4 cloves garlic	The kabobs can also be cooked
8 button mushrooms	in a nonstick skillet.

Method

Combine the flour and baking powder and sift into a bowl. Add the rest of the ingredients for the dough. Knead the dough rapidly to form a smooth mixture, first using a hand-mixer with the beater attachment, then with a dough hook. Wrap in aluminum foil and leave in a cool place for at least one hour.

To make the filling: dice the ham and put the cubes in a bowl together with dill and rice. Peel and chop the onion and sauté it lightly in butter.

Wash the mushrooms, chop them finely, and add to the onions. Fry on high heat until the liquid has evaporated. Add this to the ham, season with salt and pepper, and stir well.

Roll out the dough to a thickness of ⅛ inch/5mm and cut out 4-in/10cm circles. Put a teaspoon of filling on each. Brush the edges of the dough with egg white, fold over to create half-circles and press the edges tightly with the tines of a fork to prevent the filling escaping.

Place in a greased baking pan on on a cookie sheet lined with nonstick baking paper. Beat the egg yolk with milk and brush this over the pasties. Transfer to the oven.

Ingredients

For the dough

1¼ cups all-purpose flour

1 tsp baking powder

½ tsp salt

⅓ cup cold butter

5 tbsp sour cream

1 egg

For the filling

8oz/225g cooked ham

3 tbsp finely chopped dill

4 tbsp boiled rice (4 tsp raw rice)

1 onion; 1 tbsp butter

1¼ cups button mushrooms

freshly ground pepper; salt

1 egg

Pasties with Rice and Ham

Oven

Conventional oven: 375-400°F/190–200°C (preheated)

Fan-assisted oven: 350-375°F/180–190°C (preheated)

Gas oven: Mark 3 (preheated)

Baking time: around 25 minutes.

Tip

Delicious with sour cream

Method

Peel and slice the bananas, sprinkle them with lemon juice, and mix with the curry powder and cooked rice.

Heat the lobster in butter for around 2 minutes, add the shrimp.

For the cocktail sauce: mix the tomato ketchup, heavy cream, and brandy, then season with salt, pepper, sugar, and Tabasco.

Place the banana rice on a preheated platter, arrange the lobster and shrimp on top, and pour the cocktail sauce over.

Lobster with Banana Rice

Ingredients

For the banana rice	For the cocktail sauce
2 small bananas; 1-2 tbsp lemon juice	1-2 tbsp tomato ketchup
2 tsp curry powder	½ cup heavy cream
⅔ cup cooked rice grains	1 tbsp brandy
5oz/145g frozen lobster defrosted and cooked	salt; freshly ground pepper; sugar
2 tbsp butter; ⅔ cup bay shrimp	a few drops Tabasco

Method

Wash the mussels thoroughly, discarding any that are open. Heat them in a deep pot with some water.

Discard any mussels that fail to open. Remove the flesh from the opened ones.

Peel and chop the onions. Heat the oil and butter in a skillet and fry the chopped onions until they are translucent.

Add the rice and cook for 2 minutes. Add the brandy and broth, then bring to boil. Simmer for around 20 minutes on low heat, or until the rice is cooked.

Add the seafood and heavy cream and bring back to a boil. Season with pepper and salt and mix in the Parmesan cheese.

Ingredients

5 cups mussels

1 small onion

6 tbsp olive oil

3 tbsp butter

2 cups round-grain rice

1 cup white wine

3 cups beef broth

1¾ cups scampi (fresh or frozen, without shells)

1¾ cups bay shrimp (fresh or frozen, without shells)

1 cup heavy cream

1⅓ cups grated Parmesan cheese

freshly ground pepper

salt

Rice with Seafood

Method

Bring the rice, vegetable broth, and saffron to a boil. Wash the mild dry chili pepper, cut it in half, deseed, discard the ribs, and add to the pot. Cover the pot and simmer over low heat for around 20 minutes or until the rice is cooked.

Peel and quarter the apple, remove the core and cut into smaller pieces. Wash the green onions and cut them into rings. Mix the raisins, green onions, and apple into the rice and add a pinch of salt.

Blanch the banana leaves for around 5 minutes, rinse them with cold water, and drain. Cut them into 8-in/20cm squares. Take 15 pieces, pat them dry and brush the inner side with oil. With damp hands, place the rice on top, pressing it into a cake. Fold the banana leaves over it and secure with wooden cocktail sticks.

To make the sauce: peel and mince the onions and garlic and sauté them in the melted butter. Peel and chop the ginger, rinse the lemongrass, chop the thick stems, and add to the skillet.

Wash the mild dry chili peppers, cut them in half, deseed them and discard the ribs and cook with the mixture. Add the sugar and curry powder. Add the coconut milk, and bring to a boil. Season with salt.

Broil the rice packages under medium heat for around 8-10 minutes.

Serve with the coconut sauce.

Rice Packages in Coconut Sauce

Ingredients

1 cup sticky rice; 1¾ cups vegetable broth

pinch of saffron

3 large dried red chili peppers

2 apples; 1 bunch green onions (scallions)

7 tbsp raisins; salt

2 large banana leaves

oil for greasing

For the sauce

4 tbsp butter; 2 shallots; 3 cloves garlic

1-in/2.5cm piece root ginger

2 sprigs lemongrass

2 dried mild chili peppers

1 tbsp brown sugar

1 tsp curry powder

1 tbsp all-purpose flour; 1¾ cups coconut milk

Method

Peel and grate the onion. Melt the butter and fry the onion, add the rice, and fry until glazed, stirring frequently.

Mix the crème fraîche and dried herbs with enough broth to make 2 cups. Add to the rice, bring to boil, and leave to simmer for around 20 minutes.

Cut the green parts from the green onions back by around 4-6 inches, rinse and slice thinly. Clean the chanterelles or oyster mushrooms, wash if necessary, and halve or quarter the larger mushrooms. Cut into strips.

Melt the butter, fry the green onions, add all mushrooms, and season to taste. Add the peas, cover the pan, and stew for 5-7 minutes.

Stir in the boiled rice and parsley. Season to taste before serving.

Ingredients

1 onion	1 bunch green onions (scallions)
1 tbsp butter	2 cups chanterelles or oyster mushrooms
1 cup long-grain rice	1 tbsp butter
½ cup crème fraîche	1¾ cups frozen peas
1 tsp dried mixed herbs	1-2 tbsp minced parsley
1¾ cups vegetable broth	freshly ground pepper
	salt

Wild Mushroom **Risotto**

Tip

Serve the mushroom risotto with a beef,

game, or chicken stew.

Method

Heat the oil in a pressure cooker and fry the ground meat in it. Press the meat down using a fork.

Peel and cube the onions and add them to the ground meat. Let it fry further, season with salt, pepper, paprika powder, basil, and oregano.

Add the rice, broth, and tomato paste.

Close the pressure cooker and when a lot of steam escapes (after around 1 minute) set the regulator on position II. Cook for another 7-8 minutes, or until the second ring is visible.

Remove the pot from the heat and gradually turn down the pressure regulator. Remove the lid from the pot.

Let the liquid evaporate a little. Add the peas and reheat. Season with salt, pepper, and paprika powder.

Ingredients

2 tbsp oil	1 cup long-grain rice
1¾ cups ground mixed beef and pork	3 cups meat broth
4-5 onions	6 tbsp tomato paste
sweet paprika powder	1½ cups cooked peas
basil leaves	freshly ground pepper
oregano leaves	salt

Bologna **Rice**

Method

Peel and dice the onion into small cubes. Heat the oil and fry the onions. Add the rice, letting it boil vigorously. Add the broth, return to boil, then reduce the heat and simmer gently for around 15 minutes. Cut half the cheese into 16 slices and reserve. Cut the rest of the cheese into cubes, mix with half of the crème fraîche and half of the herbs, blending into the rice and seasoning with salt and pepper. Put the seasoned rice in a large, oiled skillet.

Wash the tomatoes, remove the stems, cut them crosswise and place them in the skillet, cut side facing up. They should touch the bottom of the skillet.

Mix the rest of the crème fraîche with the spices. Peel and crush the garlic. Sprinkle the dried mixed herbs, salt, and pepper over the tomatoes. Place a piece of the reserved cheese on each tomato half and press it lightly into the cream.

Cover the skillet with a lid and braise for around 15 minutes.

Tomatoes with Herbed Rice

Ingredients

1 onion

2 tbsp oil

1 cup long-grain rice

2 cups hot vegetable broth

1½ cups mozzarella

⅔ cup crème fraîche

2 tbsp chopped mixed herbs
(e.g., chives, basil, thyme)

freshly ground pepper

8 medium tomatoes

1-2 cloves garlic

1 tsp mixed dried herbs

salt

Method

Peel and chop the onion and garlic and sauté in the oil. Add the rice and continue cooking, adding a little broth from time to time.

Cook the rice for around 20 minutes. It should be soft but not sticky.

To make the green rice: clean the spinach, place in a saucepan and cook until it wilts, then strain. Cook the peas in water and 1 tablespoon butter for around 5 minutes. Purée the spinach and half of the peas. Mix the purée and the rest of the peas with half the rice. Season with salt and pepper.

To make the red rice: dip the tomato in boiling water (don't let it cook), rinse in cold water, skin, cut out the stem and seeds, then cut into cubes. Slice the pepper in half, remove stem, seeds, and ribs. Wash the pepper and cut into small pieces.

Heat the oil, fry the vegetables and add the rest of the rice. Season with salt and pepper. Stir the rest of the butter and the Parmesan cheese into both types of rice.

Ingredients

1 onion

1 clove garlic

4 tbsp oil

1¾ cups short-grain rice

1 cup boiling meat broth

4 cups spinach

1⅓ cups green peas

3 tbsp water

4 tbsp butter

1 beefsteak tomato

1 red bell pepper

3 tbsp oil

3 tbsp grated Parmesan cheese

Green and Red Risotto

Method

Peel and wash the carrots and celery. Cut the leek lengthwise and wash well.
Cut the green stems into thin slices. Peel and chop the onion.

Melt the butter, add the oil, and cook the vegetables for about 5 minutes.
Add the rice and continue to cook.

Add the wine and broth, and bring to a boil. Reduce the heat and simmer
for 20 minutes. Add the bean sprouts and cook for another 5 minutes.

Crumble the goat's cheese and sprinkle it over the rice.

Ingredients

2 carrots	1 tbsp oil
3 celery stalks	1 cup fragrant rice
1 leek	1 cup white wine
1 onion	1 cup vegetable broth
1 tbsp unsalted butter	⅔ cup bean sprouts
	1½ cups sharp cheddar cheese

Rice with Vegetables

Method

Bring a pot of salted water to boil, add the rice and stir well. Bring this to a rolling boil for about 20 minutes. Sieve the rice, rinse in cold water, and let it strain well. Keep the rice warm.

Peel and chop the onions, fry in melted fat until they become translucent.

Wash the bell pepper, remove the seeds and white parts, chop into pieces, and add to the onions. Season with salt and pepper. Cover the pot and simmer the contents for about 10 minutes.

Add the corn, blending in well. Bring back to a boil and cook for 5 minutes. Season again with salt and pepper. Mix everything into the rice.

Mexican Rice

Ingredients

8 cups salted water

1 cup pre-cooked long-grain rice

1 onion

2 tbsp unsalted butter or margarine

1 large red bell pepper

6 tbsp canned corn

freshly ground pepper

salt

rice entrées

Method

Put the peas in a bowl and leave to defrost. Peel and chop the onions. Heat the oil in

a skillet and fry the onions on low heat. Add the rice and salt. Add water and mix well.

Bring to a boil and cover the skillet. Let the rice cook for about

10 minutes over low heat, stirring frequently.

Mix the defrosted peas into the rice. Bring to boil and simmer for about 15 minutes.

Season with pepper. Spread the bell pepper strips over the Risi Pisi before serving.

Ingredients

1¾ cups frozen peas

1 large onion

4 tbsp olive oil

1 cup long-grained rice

4 cups water

strips of bell pepper

freshly ground pepper

salt

Risi Pisi

Tip

Garnish the Risi Pisi with plenty of minced parsley.

Method

Strain the bamboo shoots in a colander and slice them into matchstick sized strips. Peel and wash the carrots and cut them into matchstick sized strips. Slice the leek in half, wash, and cut into rings. Wash the mushrooms, strain and cut into matchstick sized strips.

Cut the pepper in half and remove the stem, pits, and ribs. Wash and cut into strips. Shred, wash, and drain the cabbage. Peel and mince the garlic.

Coat a wok with oil, heat the oil and fry the garlic. Beat the eggs and add them gradually to the wok with the rice. Stir-fry for about 1 minute. Add the vegetable strips and bean sprouts and fry for about 3 minutes.

Season the dish with ketjap or soy sauce, salt, sugar, pepper, and monosodium glutamate if desired. Continue stir-frying for about 1 minute and serve hot.

Oriental Fried Rice

Ingredients

2oz/50g canned bamboo shoots

4 carrots; 3 leeks

2 fresh Chinese mushrooms (shiitake)

1 red bell pepper

1 small Chinese (Napa) cabbage

1 clove garlic

6 tbsp oil

1-2 eggs

2 cups boiled rice

2oz/50g fresh bean sprouts

3 tbsp ketjap (Indonesian soy sauce) or soy sauce

1 tsp salt

1⅓ tbsp sugar

½ tsp pepper

1 tsp monosodium glutamate (optional)

Method

Soak the wild rice for around 2 hours in cold water.

Peel and chop the shallot. Melt the butter and oil in a large skillet, fry the shallot until it is translucent. Add the white wine and simmer for 5 minutes.

Add the strained wild rice and risotto rice and ½ cup chicken broth. Let the broth completely evaporate before adding another ½ cup broth. Continue until all the broth has been used up.

Wash the asparagus. Do not slice them, only trim about ¼ in/0.5cm from the bottom of the stalks. Wash the morels or other wild mushrooms thoroughly, cut them in half length-wise, blanch them in boiling water, and let cool. Fry them on low heat in butter, stirring constantly, for 5 minutes.

Add the morels and asparagus to the rice and cook for 3 minutes. Remove the risotto from the heat and mix the rest of the butter and Parmesan cheese into the rice. Season with salt and pepper.

Ingredients

6 tbsp wild rice

1 shallot

3 tbsp unsalted butter

1 tbsp olive oil

5 tbsp white wine

6 tbsp risotto rice

2½ cups chicken broth

7oz/200g green asparagus

1oz/30g fresh morels (or other fresh wild mushrooms)

1 tsp unsalted butter

4 tbsp freshly grated Parmesan cheese

freshly ground pepper, salt

Asparagus Risotto with Morels

Method

Rinse the meat, pat it dry and cut it into pieces. Combine the yogurt, lemon juice, and fennel. Pour the mixture over the meat, cover, and marinate overnight. Thoroughly rinse the rice, soak for one hour, and leave to drain in a colander. Thoroughly clean the spinach, leave to drain, and chop coarsely. Melt 1 tablespoon of the clarified butter in a large skillet. Add the rice, cardamom, cinnamon, and bay leaf. Fry the rice for around 5 minutes or until glazed, stirring frequently.

Drain the meat in a colander and pour the yogurt marinade over the rice. Add enough broth to cover the rice by 1 inch.

Bring the rice to boil, boil for a few seconds, add salt, and stir the spinach into the mixture. Transfer the rice to a covered dish and place in the oven (see opposite for temperatures and baking time).

Melt the rest of the clarified butter and brown the meat all over. Stir in the rice and cook for 10 minutes or until done. Toast the pine nuts in a skillet and sprinkle them over the pilaf. Rinse and slice the tomatoes, and use them to garnish the pilaf.

Ingredients

1lb 10oz/750g lean boneless lamb

1¾ cups thickset plain yogurt

1 untreated lemon

juice squeezed

10 finely chopped fennel leaves

1 cup long-grain rice

1⅓ cups spinach

2 tbsp clarified butter

7 green cardamom pods

1 cinnamon stick

2 bayleaves

4 cups meat broth

2 tbsp pine nuts

3 tomatoes

salt

Lamb Pilaf

Oven

Conventional oven: 400°F/200°C (preheated)

Fan-assisted: 375°F/190°C (preheated)

Gas oven: Mark 3-4 (preheated)

Ready in 15 minutes.

Method

Cook the rice in salted water for about 20 minutes, strain, and keep warm. While it is cooking, slice the peppers in half; remove the stems, seeds, and ribs. Wash and dice the peppers. Peel and mince the shallots. Dice the ham.

Rinse the chicken under cold running water, pat dry, and cut into strips.

Heat the oil and stir-fry the chicken strips; season them with salt and pepper. Remove from the skillet or wok and keep warm. Fry the chopped vegetables in the same oil until they are light brown. Add the diced ham and chicken broth and simmer for about 10 minutes. Mix all the other ingredients with the rice, adding the chicken last, and season with salt, pepper, and chili sauce.

Jambalaya

Ingredients

1 cup long-grain rice

3 cups salted water

2 red bell peppers

2 green bell peppers

2 shallots

4oz/115g raw ham

6 skinless chicken breast fillets (about 8oz/250g)

4 tbsp oil; salt

freshly ground pepper

1 cup chicken broth

a few drops of mild chili sauce

Tip

Garnish the dish with a few slices of raw bell pepper

and rolled slices of ham.

Method

Rinse the lamb in cold running water and drain well. Cut the meat into bite-sized pieces and season well with salt and pepper. Heat the clarified butter in a skillet; dip the cloves of garlic in salt and sauté them. Add the meat to the garlic butter and stir-fry it in the skillet.

Add 2 cups of the broth then add the bayleaf, thyme, and rosemary. Cook on moderate heat for 20-25 minutes or until done. Rinse the rice and drain well. Add the rice to the meat and season well with salt, pepper, and cayenne pepper. Stir in the tomato paste and paprika powder. Cook the rice on moderate heat for about 20-25 minutes, adding more broth if necessary.

Season again when the rice is cooked. Transfer it to a serving platter and serve with minced parsley.

Serving suggestion

A mixed salad.

Spicy Rice with Lamb

Ingredients

1¼ lb/575g lean boneless lamb

salt; freshly ground pepper

4 tbsp clarified butter

1 tsp salt

2 cloves garlic, peeled and chopped

1 mild chili pepper, deseeded

2 onion; 1 carrot; 1 leek

about 3 cups vegetable or lamb broth

1 bayleaf; 1 sprig thyme

1 sprig rosemary

2 cups rice

pinch of cayenne pepper

2 tbsp tomato paste

1 tbsp paprika powder

1 bunch parsley

Method

Rinse, pat dry, and cut the pork into cubes. Scald the tomatoes in boiling water (do not let them cook), and rinse them in cold water. Skin, remove the cores and cut them into quarters. Wash the peppers and cut them into pieces. Peel and slice the onions.

Dice the bacon and sauté in melted fat with the pork, allowing them to brown. Add the onions and peppers and continue to fry for about 10 minutes. Season with salt, pepper, tomato paste, Tabasco, sweet paprika powder, and cayenne pepper. Add the basil and lovage leaves.

Add the beef broth and simmer for about 15 minutes. Add the tomatoes, rice, and water and cook for another 30 minutes.

Pork and Rice Medley

Ingredients

1lb/450g lean pork fillet	2 tbsp tomato paste
1¼ lb/575g tomatoes	Tabasco; sweet paprika powder
2 large bell peppers, 1 red, 1 green	cayenne pepper
2 large onions	chopped basil leaves
3 slices bacon	a few lovage leaves
4 tsp unsalted butter or margarine; salt	1 cup meat broth
freshly ground pepper	1 cup long-grain rice
	2 cups water

Method

Cook the rice in salted boiling water for 20 minutes, or until tender. Strain the rice.

Rinse the chicken in cold water, pat dry, slice lengthwise into four pieces, and then into thin strips.

Fry the chicken slowly in two batches. Season with salt, remove from the heat, and keep warm.

Pour the heavy cream into a heavy-based pan, add the broth, and a crushed garlic clove. Season with salt and saffron and reduce the heat.

Wash the pepper, cut it into quarters, and remove the stem, seeds, and white ribs. Slice the pepper into strips and add to the sauce, then cook for about 5 minutes. Warm the olives in the sauce, add the chicken and rice, and season to taste.

Chicken and Rice

Ingredients

1 cup rice	5 tbsp chicken broth
1 lean chicken breast fillet (about 12oz/340g)	1 clove garlic
2 tbsp olive oil	1 pinch saffron
½ cup heavy cream	1 yellow bell pepper
salt	2 tbsp black olives

Method

Cook the rice in salted boiling water for 20 minutes then strain.

Peel and mince the onions and garlic. Slice the peppers in half and remove the stem, seeds, and ribs. Wash again and dice them. Wash and dry the zucchini, trim the ends, and dice.

Heat the oil and sauté the onion with the garlic, zucchini, and peppers for about 5 minutes. Add the broth and cook for another 5 minutes, then season with salt and pepper.

Stir in the rice. Strain the tuna in a sieve, flake the tuna, and add it to the rice and vegetables. Season to taste before serving.

Ingredients

⅔ cup rice

4 cups salted water

2 onions

2 cloves garlic

2 bell peppers, 1 red, 1 green

2 zucchini

4 tbsp olive oil

½ cup vegetable broth

freshly ground pepper

7oz/200g can tuna in oil

salt

Rice with Tuna and Vegetables

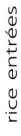

rice entrées

Method

Rinse the pork in cold running water, pat dry, and cut into cubes. Dice and fry the bacon.

Add the pork, continue cooking, and season to taste with salt and pepper.

Peel and slice the onion, add it to the skillet and brown it over moderate heat. Add the

short-grained rice, stir-fry until coated with oil, and pour in the broth.

Place the tomatoes in boiling water (do not cook), rinse under cold running water, skin, and core

them. Dice the tomatoes and add them to the rice-and-meat mixture.

Cook for around 35 minutes. Just before serving, stir in the crème fraîche, season to taste with

the paprika powder, and sprinkle with the minced parsley.

Serbian Pork and Rice

Ingredients

1¼ lb/550g lean boneless pork

2oz/56g fat bacon

2-3 onions

freshly ground pepper

salt

1 cup short-grained rice

2½ cups hot meat broth

4 medium tomatoes

2 tbsp crème fraîche

sweet paprika powder

1 tbsp minced parsley

Method

Toast the grated coconut in a dry skillet until golden, then add the water. Cover and leave to cool. Transfer the coconut to a kitchen towel and squeeze out the water. Reserve the squeezed liquid.

Peel and mince the onion and garlic, fry them in oil, add the curry powder, continue cooking for 2 minutes, then add the coconut liquid. Set aside.

Boil the rice in the chicken broth for about 10 minutes; dice the crabsticks and ginger and add them to the broth.

Reheat the rice and arrange on a serving platter. Add salt and pepper to taste.

Slice the hardboiled eggs. Skin, deseed, and dice the tomatoes. Garnish the rice with the tomato flesh.

Serving suggestion

Mixed leaf salad.

Ingredients

⅔ cup unsweetened shredded coconut

1¾ cups water

1 large onion

1 clove garlic

3 tbsp vegetable oil

2 tsp curry powder

1¾ cups basmati rice

3 cups chicken broth

8 crabsticks

3oz/85g candied ginger

2 hardboiled eggs

2 tomatoes

freshly ground pepper

salt

Basmati Rice with Crabsticks and Ginger

rice entrées

Method

Bring rice and broth to a boil. Peel the garlic clove and add it to the bayleaf and peppercorns. Tie them in a piece of cheesecloth and add to the pan. Cover the pan and cook the rice for 20 minutes or until done.

Discard the garlic clove, bayleaf, and peppercorns. Mix the rice with the currants. Rinse the pickled cucumbers and slice thinly. Slice the smoked pork. Mix both types of cream and season with cinnamon and allspice.

Put a quarter of the rice in a greased oven dish; create a layer with a third of the pickled cucumbers, smoked pork, and cream. Repeat the process until all ingredients are used.

Top with a layer of rice. Dot the the rice with butter and put the dish in the oven (see below for temperatures and time). Serve the dish piping hot with cold sour cream.

Oven

Conventional oven: 425°F/215°C (preheated)

Fan-assisted: 400°F/200°C (not preheated)

Gas oven: Mark 4-5 (not preheated)

Ready in around 50 minutes.

Herbed Rice and Pork Ribs

Ingredients

1¾ cups precooked rice	11oz/315g smoked pork ribs
2 cups boiling meat broth	1 cup sour cream
1 bayleaf	1 cup heavy cream
1 clove garlic	½ tsp ground cinnamon
4 peppercorns	pinch of chili powder
3 tbsp currants	3 tbsp unsalted butter, cut into pieces
2 cups pickled cucumbers	sour cream for serving

Method

Brush the mussels, clams, and lobster tails in cold running water, discarding any opened mussels. Put the mussels, clams, and lobster on kitchen paper to drain.

Rinse the drumsticks, pat dry, and season well with salt and pepper. Heat the oil in a skillet and sauté the drumsticks for 8-10 minutes. Remove them from the skillet and keep them warm. Fry the lobster tails lightly in the pan drippings, remove, and reserve them with the drumsticks. Peel and mince the onions and garlic and sauté in the pan drippings until translucent.

Slice the bell peppers in half, then discard the seeds and white ribs. Cut the peppers in strips and add to the onions. Wash the leek and celery stalks and cut them into thin strips. Add them to the other vegetables and fry until translucent. Add the mussels and clams, cover the pot, and let stew until they open. Discard any mussels that fail to open.

Grease a paella pan with a little oil and fry the rice into until it is translucent. Add the drumsticks, lobster tails, vegetables, and mussels. Add the white wine and broth. Season well with salt, pepper, saffron, and cayenne pepper; mix well.

Transfer the pan to the oven (See below for temperatures and time). Remove the paella from the oven, season and serve sprinkled with the spices.

Paella

Ingredients

1¾ cups mussels; ⅔ cup clams

4 lobster tails

4 chicken drumsticks

salt; freshly ground pepper

1 cup olive oil; 4 cloves garlic; 1 onion

1 red bell pepper; 1 yellow bell pepper

1 small leek

1 celery stalk; olive oil

1 cup short-grain Spanish rice

1 cup dry white wine

1 cup meat or chicken broth

pinch of saffron; cayenne pepper

½ bunch chopped fresh herbs

(e.g. parsley, basil, thyme, rosemary)

Oven

Conventional oven: 375°F/190°C (preheated)

Fan-assisted oven: 350°F/180°C (preheated)

Gas oven: Mark 2-3 (preheated)

Baking time: 25-30 minutes

Method

Bring the milk, sugar, and vanilla extract to boil. Add the rice and cook over low heat for about 30 minutes, stirring occasionally (the rice grains should remain whole).

Soften the gelatin in 1 tablespoon water and leave for around 10 minutes. Add to the cooked rice and stir until the gelatin has completely dissolved. Leave the mixture to cool.

Whip the cream until soft peaks form and stir it through the rice. Rinse a tube pan in cold water and transfer the rice to it. Refrigerate until set.

To make the apricot preserve: wash the apricots, cut them in half, and remove the pits. Simmer them for about 10 minutes with the sugar, wine, and cinnamon stick, and then add the apricot liquor. Cool slightly or chill in the refrigerator.

Unmold the rice ring onto a serving platter, garnish with lemon balm sprigs, and serve with the cooled apricot compote.

Rice Mold with Vanilla and Apricots

Ingredients

3 cups milk

6 tbsp sugar

1 tsp vanilla extract

⅔ cup short-grained (pudding) rice

2 tbsp unflavored gelatin

4 tbsp cold water

1 cup heavy cream

For the apricot preserve

3 cups dried apricots

6 tbsp sugar

½ cup white dessert wine

1 cinnamon stick

4 tbsp apricot liqueur

lemon balm leaves

Method

Cook the rice in lightly salted, boiling water for around 25 minutes, or until soft. Drain the rice in a sieve and leave to cool. Rinse and hull the strawberries and divide them in halves. Peel the bananas, slice them, and sprinkle with lemon juice.

Toast the sunflower seeds in a dry skillet. It is important not to grease the pan.

Combine the oat flakes, fruit, and rice. Beat the cream with the vanilla sugar until stiff, combine with the yogurt and flavor with honey.

Arrange the rice mixture on dessert plates and coat with the yogurt-and-cream mixture. Sprinkle with the sunflower seeds and garnish with lemon balm leaves.

Ingredients

1 cup pecan rice

pinch of salt

2 cups strawberries

2 medium bananas

2 tbsp lemon juice

3 tbsp shelled sunflower seeds

4 tbsp oat flakes

1 cup heavy cream

1 tsp vanilla sugar

⅔ cup yogurt

1-2 tbsp honey

lemon balm leaves

Granola Rice

Tip

The strawberries can be replaced

by other seasonal fruits.

Method

Bring the milk to boil with the salt, sugar, and lemon rind. Add the rice, return to boil, and then simmer over low heat for about 30 minutes. Leave the rice to cool.

Chop the pistachio nuts and candied fruits coarsely. Mix the fruits and 2 tablespoons of the nuts with the amaretto liqueur.

Peel and slice the kiwi into wedges and arrange them around the rice. Sprinkle the surface of the rice with the rest of the chopped pistachio nuts.

Empress Rice

Ingredients

2 cups milk

pinch of salt

4 tsp sugar

1 untreated lemon, rind grated

6 tbsp pudding (round-grain) rice

½ cup shelled pistachio nuts

3 tbsp candied fruits

3 tbsp amaretto liqueur

⅔ cup thick-set plain yogurt

2 kiwis

Method

Heat a skillet and add to it 4 tablespoons powdered sugar. Gradually add the rest of the powdered

sugar, and heat through for around 1 minute until the sugar starts to change color. Dip the skillet

bottom briefly in cold water. Stir in 1 tablespoon of butter and pour this mixture over the almonds.

Leave to cool in a rinsed shallow pan or dish.

Pour boiling water over the rice. Cook the milk with the saffron, a pinch of salt, and honey.

Add the rice and simmer for around 30 minutes. Add the rest of the butter and the amaretto.

Leave to cool for a moment. Stir in the egg yolks.

Crumble the marzipan and add it.

Beat the egg whites into stiff peaks and fold them into the mixture. Transfer the soufflé

to the oven. See opposite for oven temperatures and times.

Dust the hot dish with extra sifted powdered sugar.

Ingredients

⅔ cup powdered sugar

6 tbsp unsalted butter

1⅓ cups slivered almonds

⅔ cup round-grain rice

3 cups milk

½ tsp saffron

2 tbsp honey

4 tbsp amaretto liqueur

4 egg yolks

4 egg whites

salt

Additionally

unsalted butter or margarine

sifted powdered sugar

Praline Soufflé

Oven

Conventional oven: 392°F/200°C (preheated)

Fan-assisted oven: 356°F/180°C

Gas oven: Mark 3–4 (preheated)

Baking time: approx. 30 minutes

Method

Pour the milk, sugar, and salt into a saucepan and bring to a boil. Add the rice, lemon rind, and vanilla extract, then bring to a boil stirring constantly. Cook, stirring, over moderate heat for about 30 minutes.

Dilute the saffron in the water and add to the rice.

Simmer the rice for an additional 20 minutes over medium heat.

Stir in the raisins, pistachio nuts, pomegranate seeds, and rosewater.

Leave to cool and refrigerate. Serve cold, garnished with sprigs of lemon balm.

Ingredients

4 cups milk

6 tbsp sugar

pinch salt

½ cup pudding (Carolina) rice

½ untreated lemon, rind grated

1 tsp vanilla extract

2 tbsp water

pinch of saffron

⅔ cup softened white raisins

3 tbsp pistachio nuts

2 medium pomegranates

a few drops rosewater

sprigs of lemon balm

Wedding Rice

Method

Wash and strain the rice. Bring the milk to a boil with the salt and add to the rice. Return to a boil and cook for about 30 minutes (the rice grains must remain intact). Leave to cool.

Combine the pudding mix with the baking powder. Cream the butter or margarine until soft, gradually adding the sugar, vanilla sugar, almonds, eggs, lemon extract, pudding powder, and rice.

Strain the apricots and slice them in half. Rinse a tube pan and fill with half of the creamed rice. Arrange the apricots on top and cover with the rest of the creamed rice. Cover the tube pan with a sheet of aluminum foil and place it on the central shelf of a cold oven.

Ingredients

1 cup pudding rice	6 tbsp sugar
4 cups milk	2 tsp vanilla sugar
pinch salt	3 tbsp blanched ground almonds
1 package vanilla pudding powder	3 eggs
2 level tsp baking powder	2 drops lemon extract
3 tbsp unsalted butter or margarine	2 cups canned apricot halves

Rice Pudding with Apricots

rice desserts

Method

Put the milk and 2 tablespoons of the butter, lemon rind, cinnamon stick, vanilla sugar, and salt in a saucepan.

Rinse the rice under cold running water, drain well, and add to the milk. Bring the milk to boil, stirring constantly, and cook the rice over low heat for 20-25 minutes until tender. Discard the cinnamon stick and allow the rice to cool completely. Stir the pistachio nuts, pine nuts, and raisins into the rice.

Beat 6 tablespoons of the butter and sugar in a bowl. Gradually add the egg yolks and stir them through the rice. Beat the egg white until stiff and fold it into the rice. Grease an ovenproof dish or pie pan and transfer the rice mixture to it. Dot the rice with flakes of the remaining butter and set the dish in the oven. See below for oven temperatures and baking time.

Serve the rice pudding out of the oven hot or cold.

Baked Rice Pudding

Ingredients

4 cups milk; ¾ cup unsalted butter

1 tbsp grated lemon rind

1 cinnamon stick; 1 tsp vanilla sugar

¼ tsp salt; 1 cup rice

3 tbsp pistachio nuts; 3 tbsp pine nuts

⅔ cup soaked currants

6 tbsp sugar; 4 egg yolks

4 egg whites

Oven

Conventional oven: 375°F/190°C (preheated)

Fan-assisted oven: 350°F/180°C (preheated)

Gas oven: Mark 2-3 (preheated)

Baking time: 20-25 minutes

rice desserts

Method

Peel and chop the onion. Peel and wash the celery root and cut it into small pieces.

Heat the oil in a skillet and sauté the onions until they become translucent.

Add the celery root pieces and the rice and cook for 5 minutes.

Add the orange juice and rind, water, raisins, and bayleaf.

Season with pepper, nutmeg, and salt.

Bring the rice mixture to boil and cook over low heat for 15-20 minutes.

Discard the bayleaf. Season the orange rice with pepper, grated nutmeg, and salt.

Ingredients

1 onion	5 tbsp water
1 small celery root	4 tsp white raisins
1 tbsp oil	1 bayleaf
⅓ cup long-grain rice	freshly ground pepper
⅔ cup orange juice	grated nutmeg
1 tsp grated rind from an untreated orange	salt

Herbed Orange Rice

Tip

Serve with chicken fillets or

duck breast.

Index